This Journal Belongs to LAHACKER:

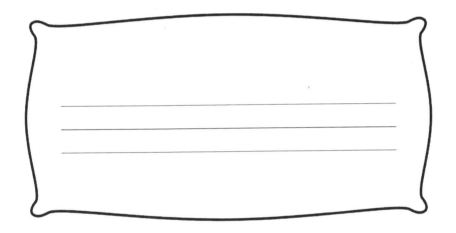

This book is dedicated to "Larry & Curly"

Love, Moe

1

About This Journal

There are so many incredible adventures to experience in Los Angeles that its pretty hard to narrow it down to just 50.

That is why we tried to recommend some of the most beloved and iconic spots. Many are famous and you may have done them already or even done them many times.

But we would still like to implore you to go out and try them again. Bring your LAHacker journal with you and fully soak in all these amazing Los Angeles gems in the moment.

Capture your experience in your LAHacker journal so you can cherish it forever. And don't forget to check it off your LA Bucket list.

CULTURE

Los Angeles is often dismissed by it's big city counterparts as having 'no culture'. Well we are here to show you that nothing could be

further from the truth. Packed with world class museums, art galleries, theaters and historical landmarks, the ethnically diverse culture of

Los Angeles is rich with the arts. Below you will find 10 of our favorite LAHacker worthy Culture spots.

Location Quick List

- LACMA
- Hsi Lai Temple
- Huntington Library
- Union Station
- The Broad

- Self Realization Lake Shrine Temple
- Watts Towers
- Bradbury Building
- Exposition Park
- City Hall/Grand Park

LACMA

The Los Angeles County Art Museum (LACMA) is the largest art museum in the Western United States. It's located in the exciting and vibrant area of Mid City LA and people come from all over to take pictures with the popular outdoor installation 'Urban Lights'.

Hack:
Every Friday night in the Summer months the LACMA holds one of the most popular free concerts in the city called 'Jazz at LACMA'. A perfect evening of free live music, with wine and a picnic on the grassy lawn.

LACMA

Date: ....

Who was I with ....

<u>My experience:</u> ....

_____

_____

_____

_____

_____

_____

_____

_____

_____

_____

_____

_____

_____

_____

L.A. Bucket List: ☐ Yes!

Experience Rating:
😕 😲 😮 🙂 😃

LACMA

LACMA

Hsi Lai Temple

The Hsi Lai Temple is a breathtaking mountain monastery in Hacienda Heights. It is one of the largest Buddhist temples in the Western Hemisphere. All are welcome to wander the grounds and seek a little peace, enlightenment and escape from the city even if just for a few hours.

Hack:
The Hsi Lai Temple serves a delicious daily vegetarian lunch at a very, very affordable price and the proceeds go to a good cause.

Hsi Lai Temple

Date: _____

Who was I with _____

My experience: _____

_____

_____

_____

_____

_____

_____

_____

_____

_____

_____

_____

_____

_____

_____

_____

L.A. Bucket List: ☐ Yes!

Experience Rating:
☹ 😲 😯 ☺ 😄

Hsi Lai Temple

Hsi Lai Temple

Huntington Library

The Huntington Library features an incredible collection of Art, Botanical Gardens and special cultural events all located on its beautiful grounds in San Marino. If you appreciate art, culture, nature, and beauty be prepared to spend the day in constant amazement.

Hack:
The Huntington Library is huge with so much to see. Plan accordingly for a long day with comfortable shoes, sunscreen, and water.

The Huntington Library

Date: _____

Who was I with _____

My experience: _____

_____

_____

_____

_____

_____

_____

_____

_____

_____

_____

_____

_____

L.A. Bucket List: ☐ Yes!

Experience Rating:
😐 😮 😵 ☺ 😛

Union Station

Los Angeles Union Station is the main railway station in LA and the largest railroad passenger terminal in the Western United States. It first opened in 1939 and holds on to those historic romantic vibes of the past with its beautiful mix of Art Deco and Spanish Colonial Revival architecture.

Hack:
Union Station is worth the visit just to appreciate the beautiful history and architecture. But it also has a massive brewery called Imperial Western, frequently holds exciting unique events and is walking distance to Olvera Street and Chinatown.

Union Station

Date: _____

Who was I with _____

My experience: _____

_____

_____

_____

_____

_____

_____

_____

_____

_____

_____

_____

_____

_____

_____

L.A. Bucket List: ☐ Yes!

Experience Rating:

😕 😮 😯 🙂 😃

Union Station

Union Station

The Broad

The Broad is a contemporary art museum on Grand Avenue in Downtown Los Angeles. First opened in September 2015 The Broad has done much to disprove the silly notion that Los Angeles has no culture. As of now, general admission to The Broad is free and they only charge for special exhibitions.

Hack:
The Broad is free and accepts walk-ups but we recommend you reserve a time slot online ahead of time. There is no telling how long you will be waiting in line if you just show up.

The Broad

Date: _____

Who was I with _____

My experience: _____

_____

_____

_____

_____

_____

_____

_____

_____

_____

_____

_____

_____

_____

_____

L.A. Bucket List: ☐ Yes!

Experience Rating:
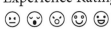

The Broad

The Broad

Lake Shrine Self-Realization

Lake Shrine Self-Realization is a meditation garden and spiritual oasis with a pond, walking grounds a windmill and more. This gorgeous garden is available to anyone who wants a quick escape from the urban chaos for peace, quiet and self-reflection. It is located right off busy Sunset Boulevard in the Pacific Palisades.

Hack:
Though it was founded and dedicated by Paramahansa Yogananda in 1950, the Shrine is open to all faiths and religions. They even have open faith service at their temples that anyone can attend.

Lake Shrine Self-Realization

Date: _____

Who was I with _____

My experience: _____

_____

_____

_____

_____

_____

_____

_____

_____

_____

_____

_____

_____

_____

L.A. Bucket List: ☐ Yes!

Experience Rating:
😐 😲 😵 😊 😀

Lake Shrine Self-Realization

Lake Shrine Self-Realization

The Watts Towers

The Watts Towers or Towers of Simon Rodia, are one of the most stunning and improbable works of public art anywhere in the United States. A fascinating urban art piece, its a collection of 17 massive sculptural towers, meticulously hand constructed by one person over the course of 34 years.

Hack:
The entire sculpture is outdoors, you can show up any time to take a look at it. But it's surrounded by a fence and a locked gate, so if you want an insiders look along with background on all the fascinating history you'll need to visit during one of their guided tours.

The Watts Towers

Date: _____

Who was I with _____

My experience: _____

_____

_____

_____

_____

_____

_____

_____

_____

_____

_____

_____

_____

_____

_____

_____

_____

L.A. Bucket List:　☐ Yes!

Experience Rating:
😐 😮 😲 🙂 😃

The Watts Towers

The Watts Towers

The Bradbury Building

The Bradbury Building is an architectural landmark in downtown Los Angeles. Best known for its extraordinary skylight atrium, the light-filled Victorian vibes has made it a popular set for movies like Blade Runner in the past and the Instagram influencers of the present.

Hack:
The Bradbury Building is free for you to walk around the lower levels during normal hours. But if you love architecture and want to know more about the history of this iconic LA Landmark you can book a DTLA walking tour with the Los Angeles Conservatory.

The Bradbury Building

Date: _____

Who was I with _____

My experience: _____

_____

_____

_____

_____

_____

_____

_____

_____

_____

_____

_____

_____

_____

_____

_____

_____

L.A. Bucket List: ☐ Yes!

Experience Rating:
😐 😮 😯 🙂 😁

The Bradbury Building

The Bradbury Building

Exposition Park

Exposition Park is home to some of Los Angeles most iconic museums, sports facilities, recreational areas, and cultural institutions. It is jam-packed with activities that include the California African-American Museum, the California Science Center, The Exposition Rose Garden, LA Memorial Coliseum, The Natural History Museum, the Banc of California Stadium and more!

Hack:
Spending a day exploring all that Exposition Park has to offer can be exhausting. Refuel at the amazing new upscale Food Hall called The Fields LA. Packed with eateries, activities and a bar it is an LA foodies dream.

Exposition Park

Date:

Who was I with

My experience:

L.A. Bucket List: ☐ Yes!

Experience Rating:
😐 😲 😮 😊 😄

Exposition Park

Exposition Park

Grand Park

Grand Park is a dynamic urban outdoor park in the heart of DTLA that has quickly become one of the cultural centerpieces for Angelenos to gather and celebrate. The park is open to the public every day from 5:30 a.m. to 10:00 p.m. and is located near many other Downtown attractions like The Music Center, City Hall, The Broad, and Disney Concert Hall.

Hack:
Grand Park is one of the main gathering places in the city for major events like New Years Eve celebrations and July 4th firework shows. They also have a constant stream of fun, live events all year long so be sure to check their calendar to catch the action.

Grand Park

Date: _____

Who was I with _____

My experience: _____

_____

_____

_____

_____

_____

_____

_____

_____

_____

_____

_____

_____

_____

_____

L.A. Bucket List: ☐ Yes!

Experience Rating:
☹ 😲 😯 ☺ 😄

Grand Park

Grand Park

ℰ𝒜𝒯𝒮

A tour through the City of Angels will make you feel like you died and went to foodie heaven. From diverse ethnic,

to celebrity chef owned, to legendary hole in the walls, to Michelin star, and new experimental fusion, Los Angeles

has without a doubt some of the best food choices in the world. In this list you will find 10 legendary places to eat in LA.

Location Quick List

- Grand Central Market
- Philippe the Original

- Little Ethiopia
- Smorgsasburg

- The San Gabriel Valley
- Roscoe's Chicken and Waffles

- Olvera Street
- In-n-Out

- Yamashiro
- Koreatown

Grand Central Market

For about a century Grand Central
Market has served as the go-to food
hall for the hungry and eclectic
Downtown LA crowd. But it has
become much more hip and upscale
in recent years thanks to a massive
modernization back in 2012 that is
credited with helping all of DTLA
in its revitalization.
Now you will find dozens of
modern and up and coming food &
drink vendors mixed with the
classics making the Grand Central
Market easily live up to the
legendary foodie status it enjoys
today.

Hack:
Grand Central Market is an amazing
location Downtown. Be sure to ride
the historic Angels Flight railway,
tour the Bradbury Building, and
visit La Catedral De Los Angeles. All
of them are very close by.

Grand Central Market

Date:
_____

Who was I with
_____

My experience:
_____

_____

_____

_____

_____

_____

_____

_____

_____

_____

_____

_____

_____

L.A. Bucket List: ☐ Yes!

Experience Rating:
😐 😲 😳 🙂 😄

Grand Central Market

Grand Central Market

Little Ethiopia

Little Ethiopia on Fairfax is only about one block long but it's jam-packed with delicious and authentic East African eateries. Ethiopian food revolves around injera - a spongy bread that's used to roll, dip, and scoop every last bite of whatever yummy thing you ordered. And no matter what you order it is very likely to be crazy delicious, healthy, affordable and fun.

Hack:
Ethiopian food is a different and experiential experience. The food is traditionally eaten with your hands so leave your inhibitions and hang-ups at the door and you will have much more fun.

Little Ethiopia

Date:

Who was I with

My experience:

L.A. Bucket List: ☐ Yes!

Experience Rating:
😐 😮 😲 😊 😁

Little Ethiopia

Little Ethiopia

The San Gabriel Valley

Real LA foodies know that the best Asian food in LA without a doubt is in the San Gabriel Valley. An embarrassment of Asian culinary riches, the SGV goes far beyond the Americanized Chinese fare usually offered to us. The San Gabriel Valley is famous for authentic specialties from across the Asian continent including India, Indonesia, Vietnam, and Taiwan and at affordable prices.

Hack:
If you love Dim Sum the San Gabriel Valley has you covered. Without a doubt, some of the best Dim Sum restaurants you can find in California is waiting in the SGV. Just make sure you bring someone who knows what they are doing when it comes to Dim Sum. The meal will be cheaper and tastier!

The San Gabriel Valley

Date: _____

Who was I with _____

My experience: _____

_____

_____

_____

_____

_____

_____

_____

_____

_____

_____

_____

_____

_____

_____

_____

L.A. Bucket List: ☐ Yes!

Experience Rating:
😐 😲 😳 🙂 😁

The San Gabriel Valley

The San Gabriel Valley

Olvera Street

Olvera Street is often called "the birthplace of Los Angeles," and is a loving tribute to Mexican culture with an authentic Marketplace that recreates a romantic "Old Los Angeles". About a block-long, the narrow, tree-shaded, brick-paved market has rustic structures, classic street vendors, cafes, restaurants, and gift shops. There are so many amazing places to get a Taco in LA but because of the history, we are recommending you do it at Olvera Street.

Hack:
Olvera street is awesome. Not only can you enjoy hours exploring this DTLA classic you can also hit up other nearby downtown historic gems. Just a few minutes walk away is Chinatown, Union Station, Philippe French Dip and more.

Olvera Street

Date:

Who was I with

My experience:

L.A. Bucket List: ☐ Yes!

Experience Rating:
☺ ☺ ☺ ☺ ☺

Olvera Street

Olvera Street

Yamashiro

Towering 250 feet above
Hollywood Boulevard, this historic
LA landmark high in the
Hollywood Hills has welcomed
guests for generations. The one of a
kind dining experience offers
striking views of the city, along
with its beautiful gardens,
remarkable architecture, and even
a Koi pond.

Hack:
As if eating at Yamashiro's wasn't
cool enough they found a way to
make a visit even more
memorable. On Thursday
evenings during the Summer
months, they have a special
Farmers Night Market. A magical
event of tasting and drinking with
the lights of Hollywood
illuminating the sky as far as you
can see.

Yamashiro

Date: _____

Who was I with _____

My experience: _____

_____

_____

_____

_____

_____

_____

_____

_____

_____

_____

_____

_____

L.A. Bucket List: ☐ Yes!

Experience Rating:
😐 😮 😲 😊 😁

Yamashiro

Yamashiro

Philippe the Original French Dip

Philippe's is a historic and unique deli most famous for serving up the sandwich they claim to have created, their signature French dip. Philippes has been open since 1908 and they do their best to keep the old school classic charm with low prices and much of their original menu and vibe.

Hack:
We are so spoiled in Los Angeles we have 2 places that claim to have invented the French Dip Sandwich! Coles also opened in 1908 and has long proclaimed they first created the icon sandwich, not Phillipe's. You can try both and see which you like best.

Philippe the Original

Date:

Who was I with

My experience:

L.A. Bucket List: ☐ Yes!

Experience Rating:
😐 😮 😵 😊 😁

Philippe the Original

Smorgasburg

Hidden in a huge back lot at the
ROW DTLA, is a foodie lover
dream spot called Smorgasburg.
Dozens of the best food trucks in
the city get together every Sunday
to delight us with their inspiring
and tasty culinary creations.

Hack:
Smorgasburg is held every Sunday
at the ROW DTLA and this is
when you will find the most
people there. But the ROW DTLA
has become a great foodie
destination on its own with its
permanent restaurants. Be sure to
visit on a non-Sunday to enjoy
some of these amazing eateries
without all the Smorgasburg
crowds.

Smorgasburg

Date: _____

Who was I with _____

My experience: _____

_____

_____

_____

_____

_____

_____

_____

_____

_____

_____

_____

_____

_____

_____

_____

L.A. Bucket List: ☐ Yes!

Experience Rating:
😐 😲 😵 😊 😁

Smorgasburg

Smorgasburg

Roscoe's Chicken and Waffles

Chicken and Waffles are everywhere nowadays but Roscoe's House of Chicken and Waffles is the original cult classic that made this odd pairing popular in Los Angeles. It was founded in 1975 and is best known, of course, for their famous chicken and waffles, but they also have a full menu of more traditional items.

Hack:
Roscoe's is a beloved local eatery and busy at all 7 locations. But if you want to go to the 'hotspot' one and where you are most likely see a celebrity try the location on Gower in Hollywood.

Roscoe's Chicken and Waffles

Date: _____

Who was I with _____

My experience: _____

_____

_____

_____

_____

_____

_____

_____

_____

_____

_____

_____

_____

_____

_____

_____

L.A. Bucket List: ☐ Yes!

Experience Rating:

Roscoe's Chicken and Waffles

Roscoe's Chicken and Waffles

In-n-Out

In-n-Out is a nostalgic and beloved burger joint for anyone who grew up in Southern California. West coasters rave about In-n-Outs tasty fresh ingredients, simple environment, cheap prices and of course that secret order menu! If you are just visiting LA you may wonder what all the fuss is about but just go with it and trust it's an LA lunch stop you have to make at least once.

Hack:
There are In-n-Outs all over LA but our favorite is next to LAX on Sepulveda. Right by a grass park you can grab your food and picnic as landing planes roar right above your head. They are so close it almost feels like you can reach out and touch them.

In-n-Out

Date: _____

Who was I with _____

My experience: _____

_____

_____

_____

_____

_____

_____

_____

_____

_____

_____

_____

_____

_____

_____

L.A. Bucket List:　☐ Yes!

Experience Rating:
☺ ☺ ☺ ☺ ☺

In-n-Out

In-n-Out

Koreatown

We have so many delicious Asian food choices in Los Angeles its ridiculous. But Koreatown is something special. It's not just the incredibly authentic and tasty food like Korean BBQ, Kimchi, and Bulgogi its the whole scene. The vibrant district of KTown will make you feel like you have transported out of LA and right into the heart of Seoul.

Hack:
Korea Town is known for amazing food but there is much more to experience in the culture. KTown comes alive after dark with the best night life in the city. Where else can you eat Korean BBQ, do Karaoke, and get a spa treatment at 1A.M.?

Koreatown

Date:

Who was I with

My experience:

L.A. Bucket List: ☐ Yes!

Experience Rating:
😐 😮 😲 😊 😁

Koreatown

Koreatown

OUTDOORS

The almost year round mild sunny weather of Los Angeles ensures people spend plenty of time outdoors enjoying it.

With the beautiful beaches for swimming and surfing, the marvelous trails for hiking and biking LA is an active persons outdoor paradise.

Check off some of the most amazing nature activities in Los Angeles with our 10 favorite outdoor spots.

Location Quick List

- Runyon Canyon
- Silverlake Stairs
- The Strand
- Venice Canals
- Angels Point
- WaterFalls
- The Hollywood Sign
- The Wisdom Tree
- Malibu
- Stand Up Paddle Board

Runyon Canyon

They call it "Runway" Canyon for a reason. You will find some of the most attractive people in Los Angeles sweating it out at this popular Hollywood Hills hiking spot.

But it's not just the scenery that draws hundreds each day. Runyon Canyon Park is a beautiful 160-acre park with some of the city's best trails and boasts spectacular views of Los Angeles.

Hack:

Have a dog? This park and hiking hotspot is especially loved by dog-owners since they can hike the trails with their four-legged friends without a leash as long as the dogs are not aggressive.

Runyon Canyon

Date:

Who was I with

My experience:

L.A. Bucket List: ☐ Yes!

Experience Rating:
😕 😯 😲 🙂 😃

Runyon Canyon

Runyon Canyon

The Strand

Everyone calls it "The Strand" but the official name of this amazing paved bicycle path that runs mostly along the Pacific Ocean shoreline in Los Angeles is The Marvin Braude Bike Trail.

The Strand starts at Will Rogers State Beach and travels through all of the South Bay beach communities and 2 harbors: Marina del Rey and King Harbor at Redondo Beach. A full ride can be as far as 40 miles long!

Hack:
Some people that ride The Strand are hardcore bikers who want the full 40 miles. We prefer the casual ride between Manhattan Beach and Redondo Beach stopping along the way for eats and drinks.

The Strand

Date: _____

Who was I with _____

My experience: _____

_____

_____

_____

_____

_____

_____

_____

_____

_____

_____

_____

_____

_____

_____

_____

_____

L.A. Bucket List: ☐ Yes!

Experience Rating:
😐 😮 😲 🙂 😃

The Strand

The Strand

Angels Point

Reach for the heavens while taking in spectacular one of a kind views of Los Angeles at Elysian Park and the 'secret swing' on top of Angels Point.

There are many amazing vantage points above the city to take in all its massive and breathtaking beauty. But Angels Point in Elysian Park near Dodger Stadium offers a rewarding adventure and a unique surprise after the short but steep hike to the top.

There you will find a "secret swing" to enjoy peacefully in the clouds high above all the craziness of the City of Angels.

Hack:
At times the secret swing is ripped down. Make sure its up before going. To do that go on Instagram. Search "secret swings". Be sure there are very recent posts of this swing before heading out.

Angels Point

Date:

Who was I with

My experience:

L.A. Bucket List: ☐ Yes!

Experience Rating:
☺ ☺ ☺ ☺ ☺

Angels Point

Angels Point

The Hollywood Sign

Take an adventurous hike with maybe the best pay off ever. A close up selfie with the iconic Hollywood sign in the background. The Hollywood sign is one of Los Angeles most famous landmarks and the hike up to it is a fun and beautiful way to spend a day.

Hack:
There are generally 3 hiking routes to take but one of the best for pictures is to hike up and behind the sign. To find the trailhead that leads you there go to 3200 Canyon Dr, Los Angeles, CA, 90068

The Hollywood Sign

Date:

Who was I with

My experience:

L.A. Bucket List: ☐ Yes!

Experience Rating:

☺ 😮 😲 ☺ 😄

The Hollywood Sign

The Hollywood Sign

Malibu

Miles and miles of freeway down Highway 1, sometimes moving at a crawl, can make a trip to Malibu seem like a world away. But it is so worth it. That drive will take you down one of the most scenic and beautiful stretches in all of Southern California.

When you get to Malibu you will have so many amazing destinations to choose from, Zuma Beach, the Malibu Pier, Malibu Farmers Market, Paradise Cove, Malibu Wines and many more.

Hack:
Arguably the most beautiful beach in Malibu is El Matador State Beach. The natural caves and rock formations along the shore create an atmosphere that looks like a scene from a romantic movie making this beach a magnet for photoshoots.

Malibu

Date:

Who was I with

My experience:

L.A. Bucket List: ☐ Yes!

Experience Rating:
☺ 😮 😲 ☺ 😃

Malibu

Malibu

Silverlake Stairs

Called the 'Stairway Capital of LA'
the hilly neighborhood of
Silverlake has multiple sets of steep
stairs proving Los Angeles wasn't
always just a car town.

Climbing the Hidden Staircases of
Silverlake is one of the most
popular ways to get an outdoor
workout and also to get some epic
pics for the Gram. That is because
some of the staircases are painted
with bright colors and gorgeous
murals.

Hack:
There any many beautiful
staircases in Silverlake. But by far
the most popular is the
'Micheltorena Stairs'. Do a search
on Instagram and you will find
hundreds of pictures of people
posing with the beautiful heart
painted staircase.

Silverlake Stairs

Date: _____

Who was I with _____

My experience: _____

_____

_____

_____

_____

_____

_____

_____

_____

_____

_____

_____

_____

_____

L.A. Bucket List: ☐ Yes!

Experience Rating:
😐 😮 😲 🙂 😄

Silverlake Stairs

Silverlake Stairs

Venice Canals

The Venice Canal Historic District is an area in the Venice section of Los Angeles. There you will find breathtakingly beautiful man-made canals that were built in 1905 by developer Abbot Kinney as part of his plan to bring the charm of Venice, Italy to LA.

The Venice Canals are in a peaceful neighborhood surrounded by homes but you are free to walk the path and the bridge and appreciate the picturesque beauty.

Hack:
The Venice Canals are not really meant for you to get on the water and you will not find any kayak or SUP rentals. But very close by in Marina Del Rey is Mothers Beach one of the most popular places in Los Angeles for kayaking and SUP.

Venice Canals

Date:

Who was I with

My experience:

L.A. Bucket List: ☐ Yes!

Experience Rating:

Venice Canals

Venice Canals

Waterfalls

We are fortunate in Los Angeles to have many spectacular hiking spots, like Runyon Canyon, Griffith Park, and the Baldwin Hills Scenic Overlook that are just minutes from the city.

But if you want to really get back to nature you can drive a little farther out and do a hike most people don't even know is available near LA. A hike to a Waterfall. Some of the most popular waterfall hikes are Eaton Canyon, Escondido Falls, Sturtevant Falls, and Hermit Falls.

Hack:
Because of the famous lack of rainfall in Southern California you want to time your hike right or you may just see a trickle instead of a waterfall. The best time of year to go for a full waterfall is usually during the later winter and early spring rainy season.

Waterfalls

Date:

Who was I with

My experience:

L.A. Bucket List: ☐ Yes!

Experience Rating:
☹ 😲 😮 😊 😃

Waterfalls

Waterfalls

The Wisdom Tree

Hike up a rugged trail near the heart of the city up to the spectacular Wisdom Tree via Cahuenga and Burbank Peaks. This is not the easiest hike you can take in the Griffith Park area but the payoff is huge at the top with tremendous views of Griffith Park and greater Los Angeles.

Also at the top, you will find a lone and majestic tree. Legend says the Wisdom Tree was the only tree left standing after a devastating wildfire in 2007 scorched more than 817 acres in and around Griffith Park.

Hack:
Be sure to bring a notebook and pen! Dreamers and well-wishers will write and leave a positive note in an ammo box left at the foot of the tree for future visitors to read and be inspired!

The Wisdom Tree

Date: _____

Who was I with _____

My experience: _____

_____

_____

_____

_____

_____

_____

_____

_____

_____

_____

_____

_____

_____

L.A. Bucket List: ☐ Yes!

Experience Rating:
☺ ☺ ☺ ☺ ☺

The Wisdom Tree

The Wisdom Tree

Stand Up Paddle Board

Whether you're a beginner or an experienced waterman, stand-up paddleboarding is one of LA's hottest and most popular aquatic activities.

Luckily, Angelenos are blessed with miles of sprawling shoreline from Malibu to the South Bay and in between to choose from when searching for the perfect SUP spot.

Hack:
If you are beginner in SUP do not go to the Ocean! You will want to practice on calm waters like a Marina first. Our recommendation is Marina Del Rey. Extremely calm waters to enjoy a stress-free day and also plenty of convenient spots to rent your paddleboard.

Stand Up Paddleboard

Date: _____

Who was I with _____

My experience: _____

_____

_____

_____

_____

_____

_____

_____

_____

_____

_____

_____

_____

_____

_____

L.A. Bucket List: ☐ Yes!

Experience Rating:

Stand Up Paddle Board

Stand Up Paddleboard

LANDMARKS

Los Angeles is full of landmarks that are universally recognized world wide and those that are mostly known only to locals but beloved just the same.

Whether you want to take selfies or just hang out at these famous spots here are 10 landmarks we think should be on every LAHackers bucket list.

Location Quick List

- The Getty
- The Hollywood Bowl
- The Korean Bell
- Disney Concert Hall
- Griffith Observatory

- Angels Flight
- Venice Beach Sign
- The Malibu Pier
- Santa Monica Ferris Wheel
- Hollywood Walk of Fame

The Getty

One of the most spectacular museums in Los Angeles boasts an impressive collection of classics from Van Gogh, Monet, and Cezanne. The 120-acre campus also amazes with the stunning architecture of its six buildings and its beautiful gardens.

Worth the visit alone, however, is the breathtaking views of Los Angeles from the top of the mountain that the Getty Center rests on. To visit is free but you must pay for parking before taking a tram ride up from the lot to the Getty.

Hack:
The Getty Center is actually just 1 of 2 locations for the J. Paul Getty Museum in the area. There is also the lesser-known Getty Villa in Malibu. Trading the city views for ocean views the Getty Villa is dedicated to the study of the arts and cultures of ancient Greece, Rome, and Etruria.

The Getty

Date: _____

Who was I with _____

<u>My experience:</u> _____

_____

_____

_____

_____

_____

_____

_____

_____

_____

_____

_____

_____

_____

_____

_____

L.A. Bucket List: ☐ Yes!

Experience Rating:
☹ 😮 😯 🙂 😄

The Getty

The Getty

The Hollywood Bowl

Since its opening in 1922, the iconic outdoor concert venue, the Hollywood Bowl has been the premier destination for live music in Southern California. There is nothing like listening to the stars on the stage and looking up to the stars in the sky at the Hollywood Bowl. And for most events, you can bring your own picnic and wine!

Hack:
Many people don't know that the Hollywood Bowl is actually a public park. This means that LA residents are free to roam around the park during open hours as long as there is no concert or event going on!

The Hollywood Bowl

Date: _____

Who was I with _____

My experience: _____

_____

_____

_____

_____

_____

_____

_____

_____

_____

_____

_____

_____

_____

_____

_____

_____

L.A. Bucket List: ☐ Yes!

Experience Rating:
😐 😲 😳 🙂 😁

The Hollywood Bowl

The Hollywood Bowl

The Korean Bell

Hidden at the end of the I-110
freeway in sleepy San Pedro is a
cultural gem called the Korean
Bell. The massive and intricately-
decorated bell lays in Angels Gate
Park and was donated in 1976 to
the people of Los Angeles by the
people of the Republic of Korea to
celebrate the friendship between
our countries.

Hack:
San Pedro has many amazing
things and luckily for you most
are very close to the Korean
Bell. Go check out Cabrillo
Beach, Point Fermin Park,
Crafted and the LA Waterfront
all just a few minutes away.

The Korean Bell

Date:

Who was I with

My experience:

L.A. Bucket List: ☐ Yes!

Experience Rating:
☺ 😮 😲 ☺ 😄

The Korean Bell

The Korean Bell

Disney Concert Hall

One of the most uniquely designed buildings in the world was created by famed architect Frank Gehry and sits on Grand Avenue in DTLA. It is the Walt Disney Concert Hall home to the LA Phil – one of the world's best orchestras – and is an unmatched venue for enjoying live classical, contemporary, and jazz music.

Hack:
The magnificent Disney Concert Hall is impressive in its own right but it also carries another secret gem. Hidden along the building's exterior, lies a lush garden tucked in the shadows called the Blue Ribbon Garden. If you're looking for a quiet place its the perfect spot to both appreciate and escape DTLA for a few minutes.

Disney Concert Hall

Date:

Who was I with

My experience:

L.A. Bucket List: ☐ Yes!

Experience Rating:

Disney Concert Hall

Disney Concert Hall

Griffith Observatory

Perched high atop Mount Hollywood and overlooking Los Angeles is the incredible landmark Griffith Observatory in Griffith Park. The observatory has been free since it first opened in 1935 and is one of the most popular tourist attractions in all of LA. But with a close view of the Hollywood Sign and an extensive collection of space and science-related displays it has also always been a local favorite.

Hack:
Touring the grounds and inside the building of the Observatory is amazing enough but they also hold monthly special events like All Space Considered, Sunset Walk & Talk, and a Public Star Party.

Griffith Observatory

Date:

Who was I with

My experience:

L.A. Bucket List: ☐ Yes!

Experience Rating:
😐 😲 😮 🙂 😄

Griffith Observatory

Griffith Observatory

Angels Flight

Take a short flight to the heavens on the "world's shortest railway" Angels Flight in downtown Los Angeles. This legendary, century-old funicular has been a draw for locals and tourists since the early 1900s.

The famous orange and black cars take you up and down Bunker Hill on a very steep hill that only runs one block. It no longer has the practical use it once did and now is more for a fun tourist type activity.

Hack:
Angels Flight is across the street from LA's most famous place for foodies, Grand Central Market. Make sure you stop by for some of the most amazing food choices in the city all in one spot after you get off Angels Flight.

Angels Flight

Date: _____

Who was I with _____

My experience: _____

_____

_____

_____

_____

_____

_____

_____

_____

_____

_____

_____

_____

_____

_____

_____

L.A. Bucket List: ☐ Yes!

Experience Rating:
😐 😲 😮 😊 😁

Angels Flight

Angels Flight

Venice Beach Sign

One of the most popular selfies you can take by the beach in LA is with the iconic Venice Sign. Go to 80 Winward Ave in Venice. There you can wait at the traffic light until the walk signal appears, you then have about a 30-second window to run out in front of the sign and strike the perfect pose!

Hack:
Want to capture a very unique shot with the Venice Sign? They regularly light up the sign-in different colors and designs throughout the year for special occasions like Christmas, Valentines Day or St. Patricks Day.

Venice Beach Sign

Date:

Who was I with

My experience:

L.A. Bucket List: ☐ Yes!

Experience Rating:
☺ 😲 😮 😊 😄

Venice Beach Sign

Venice Beach Sign

The Malibu Pier

A trip to Malibu is like a dream vacation that's right here in our very own backyard. And the landmark circa-1905 pier is a centerpiece to that Malibu getaway with its offering of the beach, shops, restaurants, fishing, water activities, and awesome people-watching.

Hack:
If you walk on the Malibu Pier you must work up an appetite for lunch at Malibu Farm. Its a restaurant right on the pier with delicious farm-to-table food, and some of the best views in Malibu.

The Malibu Pier

Date: _____

Who was I with _____

My experience: _____

_____

_____

_____

_____

_____

_____

_____

_____

_____

_____

_____

_____

_____

_____

_____

L.A. Bucket List: ☐ Yes!

Experience Rating:
☹ 😲 😵 ☺ 😄

The Malibu Pier

The Malibu Pier

Santa Monica Ferris Wheel

Pacific Park is an oceanfront amusement park that is right on famed Santa Monica Pier. The small park has a roller coaster and some other typical rides but by far the most iconic is the Santa Monica Ferris Wheel. As you rotate high in the sky snap some pics of the beautiful views of the Pacific Ocean, and even as far as Catalina Island on a clear day.

Hack:
You can get some great pics of the Ocean and Santa Monica while riding on the Ferris Wheel but the best might actually come from the beach and taking pics of the beautiful Wheel itself, especially at night when it's all lit up.

Santa Monica Ferris Wheel

Date:

Who was I with

My experience:

L.A. Bucket List: ☐ Yes!

Experience Rating:
☺ 😲 😮 🙂 😄

Santa Monica Ferris Wheel

Santa Monica Ferris Wheel

Hollywood Walk of Fame

Ok, the Hollywood Walk of Fame has tourist trap written all over it. Crowded, loud and crawling with star-eyed visitors most locals avoid the area like the plague. But every once in a while its cool to walk around on the craziness of Hollywood Boulevard and appreciate what makes it so special.

Hack:
The Walk of Fame has notoriously bad traffic and parking. Make it easy by riding the Red Line Metro Train. The Hollywood Highland stop drops you off right in the middle of the action. Just take the escalator up to the street level and you will be in the thick of the Hollywood Walk of Fame.

Hollywood Walk of Fame

Date: _____

Who was I with _____

My experience: _____

_____

_____

_____

_____

_____

_____

_____

_____

_____

_____

_____

_____

_____

L.A. Bucket List: ☐ Yes!

Experience Rating:
☹ 😲 😮 ☺ 😃

Hollywood Walk of Fame

Hollywood Walk of Fame

ACTIVITIES

There is such an endless amount of fun activities for Angelenos to experience and enjoy that it was hard to narrow it to just 10. But if you want unique things

to do that scream Los Angeles we think you will love our list of 10 best LAHacker activities.

Location Quick List

- Speakeasy Bars
- The Arts District

- Forever Cemetary
- Outdoor Movie

- Theme Parks
- Echo Park Lake

- Paradise Cove
- Catalina Island

- Rooftop Bar
- Dodgers Game

Speakeasy Bars

Speakeasy Bars are a modern homage to the underground establishments of the prohibition era from the 1920s when it was illegal to serve alcohol in the US. These retro spots are typically upscale and hip with "secret" entrances that get more elaborate and cool with each one that pops up.

Hack:
Initially most modern speakeasies had a 1920s vibe. But now you can find speakeasy-style bars and clubs that include retro 1980's, an underground Cuban club, an old-time style barbershop and more. Your best bet is to look up the Houston Brothers. They have the most amazing collection of secret bars and speakeasies in LA.

Speakeasy Bars

Date: _____

Who was I with _____

My experience: _____

_____

_____

_____

_____

_____

_____

_____

_____

_____

_____

_____

_____

_____

_____

L.A. Bucket List: ☐ Yes!

Experience Rating:
😐 😲 😮 😊 😁

Speakeasy Bars

Speakeasy Bars

Hollywood Forever Cemetary

The Stars live forever even after they've left our plane of existence at the Hollywood Forever Cemetary. It is the final resting place for entertainment legends and icons including George Harrison, Johnny Ramone, Jayne Mansfield, and Rudolph Valentino. You can walk and tour the grounds for free. And even though it's a spot frequently visited by tourist be sure to be respectful since you are in a cemetery.

Hack:
If you are into the macabre and spooky be sure to check out some of the special events held at the Hollywood Forever Cemetary. They include outdoor movie showings, Day of the Dead celebrations and even concerts! Don't worry the dead don't mind. Most of them would probably appreciate the entertainment spectacle of it all.

Hollywood Forever Cemetary

Date: _____

Who was I with _____

My experience: _____

_____

_____

_____

_____

_____

_____

_____

_____

_____

_____

_____

_____

_____

_____

_____

_____

_____

_____

L.A. Bucket List: ☐ Yes!

Experience Rating:
😕 😮 😲 😊 😃

Hollywood Forever Cemetary

Hollywood Forever Cemetary

Theme Parks

Everyone knows about Disneyland and Universal but the Los Angeles area has many other exciting theme parks to choose from. Make sure to hit up a few for thrilling rides, and a full day of amazing fun. A few we recommend besides the big 2 are Magic Mountain, Knotts Berry Farm, and California Adventure.

Hack:
If you love Water Rides, Los Angeles, and SoCal have you covered there as well. The two biggest and best are Knotts Soak City in Buena Park or Raging Waters in San Dimas.

Theme Parks

Date: _____

Who was I with _____

My experience: _____

_____

_____

_____

_____

_____

_____

_____

_____

_____

_____

_____

_____

_____

_____

_____

_____

_____

L.A. Bucket List: ☐ Yes!

Experience Rating:
☺ ☺ ☺ ☺ ☺

Theme Parks

Theme Parks

Paradise Cove

There are many incredible beaches to see in Malibu but there is only one you can legally bring your own beer and wine to. Yes, Paradise Cove is the only beach in all of LA County that allows you to BYOB and enjoy a drink right on the beach.

Hack:
Parking at Paradise Cove is limited and super expensive. But if you eat at their onsite restaurant they will validate parking for 4 hours for a very inexpensive fee. Honestly, the food is not that great but its definitely better to get the meal as well instead of just spending all that cash on parking.

Paradise Cove

Date: _____

Who was I with _____

My experience: _____

_____

_____

_____

_____

_____

_____

_____

_____

_____

_____

_____

_____

_____

L.A. Bucket List: ☐ Yes!

Experience Rating:
☺ ☺ ☺ ☺ ☺

Paradise Cove

Paradise Cove

Rooftop Bar

The taste of your $15 cocktail goes down much smoother when it comes with the incredible views offered by an LA rooftop. There are rooftop bars all over Los Angeles, from Hollywood to the Beaches to Downtown LA and most are upscale, trendy and awesome!

Hack:
With a wide variety of views you can get at these rooftop bars it can be hard to choose. But in our opinion, nothing beats those city views offered by the DTLA rooftop bars. And they also happen to be some of the hottest and trendiest places you can grab cocktails right now.

Rooftop Bar

Date: _____

Who was I with _____

My experience: _____

_____

_____

_____

_____

_____

_____

_____

_____

_____

_____

_____

_____

_____

L.A. Bucket List: ☐ Yes!

Experience Rating:
☹ 😮 😯 🙂 😀

Rooftop Bar

Rooftop Bar

The Arts District

The Arts District is one of the most exciting stories to come out of the total revitalization of DTLA over the past 10-15 years. What were once vacant warehouses and storefronts are now brimming with exciting bars, restaurants, coffee shops, art galleries, and innovative spaces.

Because of the blocks and blocks packed with amazing entertainment choices and beautiful murals on the walls, the Arts District is one of the best places to walk around and take all of it in.

Hack:
There are so many incredible things to do in the Arts District but you have to make sure you try Two Bit Circus. Its a one of kind spot billed as The World's First Micro-Amusement Park and features futuristic and immersive entertainment like VR, Story Rooms, Carnival Games, a Robot Bartender, Video Games, food, drinks and more.

The Arts District

Date:

Who was I with

My experience:

L.A. Bucket List: ☐ Yes!

Experience Rating:
☹ 😮 😲 🙂 😄

The Arts District

The Arts District

Outdoor Movie

Classic flicks, shown outdoors at an awesome LA location has become a beloved Summertime tradition that is here to stay. Screenings are shown on rooftops, beaches, by a cruise ship, and even inside a cemetery!

Besides the unique locations of these outdoor screenings, there are also organizations that throw large outdoor movie parties. These are more like a festival that combines the movie with live music and food trucks!

Hack:
With all the incredible locations for these outdoor screenings there is one that stands as the most unique and iconic. That is the movie screenings that take place at the famous Hollywood Cemetary. It is for sure a Los Angeles bucket list item you need to try at least once.

Outdoor Movie

Date: _____

Who was I with _____

My experience: _____

_____

_____

_____

_____

_____

_____

_____

_____

_____

_____

_____

_____

_____

L.A. Bucket List: ☐ Yes!

Experience Rating:
😐 😮 😲 🙂 😀

Outdoor Movie

Outdoor Movie

Echo Park Lake

Echo Park Lake is an oasis for people looking for some serene calm in the big city when the beach is too far. The area once neglected and with a reputation as a place to be avoided is now a must-visit for both locals and tourists alike.

One of the most popular activities at Echo Lake Park is to rent one of their paddle boats shaped like a giant Swan and take it for a relaxing cruise around the lake with its majestic fountain and beautiful view of the Downtown Los Angeles skyline.

Hack:
Echo Park Lake is a great place to bring a picnic. But if you forgot your basket make sure to stop by the small cafe right by the Paddle Boat rental. They have extremely tasty coffee, sandwiches, and small dishes.

Echo Park Lake

Date: _____

Who was I with _____

My experience: _____

_____

_____

_____

_____

_____

_____

_____

_____

_____

_____

_____

_____

_____

_____

L.A. Bucket List: ☐ Yes!

Experience Rating:
😐 😲 😯 ☺ 😁

Echo Park Lake

Echo Park Lake

Catalina Island

We are so lucky to have an unlimited amount of awesome quick road trips we can take from Los Angeles. But for one of the most popular, you won't be hitting the road at all but rather the water. That's right! Spectacular Catalina Island is only about an hour ride away via the Catalina Express ferry service.

With snorkeling, restaurants, eco-tours, zip-lining, a museum, fishing, boating, paddleboarding, kayaking and so much more you will never run out fun things to do on your weekend getaway to Catalina Island.

Hack:
The Catalina Express across the water takes about an hour to get there and is the preferred mode of travel for 99% of visitors. But if you have a special occasion coming up a bucket list once in a lifetime item would be a helicopter ride over. The ride is only about 15 minutes but the memories you will keep for a lifetime.

Catalina Island

Date: _____

Who was I with _____

My experience: _____

_____

_____

_____

_____

_____

_____

_____

_____

_____

_____

_____

_____

_____

_____

L.A. Bucket List: ☐ Yes!

Experience Rating:
😐 😲 😲 😊 😆

Catalina Island

Catalina Island

Dodgers Game

We are blessed in LA with 2 NBA teams, 2 Pro Football teams, 2 major league Soccer teams, a Hockey Team, and of course the beloved Los Angeles Dodgers.

We also have the Anaheim Angels who rebranded as The Los Angeles Angels but there really is only one baseball team for true die-hard LA baseball fans and its the Boys in Blue.

Hack:
A game at Dodger Stadium is iconic for any LA loving Angeleno. But there is a way to make it even better. If you attend a Friday night home game they have a spectacular fireworks show after the game. And they even invite fans down to watch it right on the field!

Dodgers Game

Date: _____

Who was I with _____

My experience: _____

_____

_____

_____

_____

_____

_____

_____

_____

_____

_____

_____

_____

_____

_____

_____

L.A. Bucket List: ☐ Yes!

Experience Rating:
☺ 😮 😯 🙂 😁

Dodgers Game

Dodgers Game

We have 2 goals with LifeHacksLA. To share the best of Los Angeles and to encourage people to experience it. Hopefully this journal will help inspire you to do just that.

If you would like to join the community and become an LAHacker you can find more about us at www.lifehacksla.com

We have a website, Instagram, and a Podcast all dedicated to people like you who love Los Angeles.

You can always reach out to us at contact@lifehacksla.com

Cheers,

Stefan – LifeHacksLA

Made in the USA
Las Vegas, NV
15 December 2022

62782408R00116